R.I.O.T.

RIGHTEOUS INVASION OF TRUTH

MANUAL

D0840414

R.I.O.T.

RIGHTEOUS INVASION OF TRUTH

MANUAL

CARMAN & RON LUCE

SPARROW®

Sparrow Press
Nashville, Tennessee

R.I.O.T. MANUAL

published by Sparrow Press and
distributed in Canada by Christian Marketing Canada, Ltd.

© 1995 Carman Ministries

International Standard Book Number: 0-917143-46-9

Printed in the United States of America

The authors would like to thank those who have labored in love to make this manual
happen. Thanks to Joni Jones, Penny Hollenbeck, Cindy Powell, Charity Virkler, Kathleen
Stephens and all the staff of Carman Ministries and Teen Mania Ministries for their input
and dedication to helping a young generation start a R.I.O.T.

Editor: Kathleen Stephens
Design and Production: Synergy Product Development

95   96   97   98   99 — 5   4   3   2   1

CONTENTS

Introduction

This manual will help you start a R.I.O.T.—a Righteous Invasion of Truth—in your town. We wrote it to get you ready for battle and to send you into war. Our purpose is not to tell you about a R.I.O.T., but to motivate and equip you to get a R.I.O.T. going. A R.I.O.T. makes the devil mad and brings lots of people to Christ.

Many people talk about doing something for God. They attend conferences and seminars where they talk about reaching people, but very few do anything about it. This manual is different. It gives you specific tactics to use to invade the devil's territory. It is an ACTION manual. That means that you will DO something as a result. If you read and follow the suggestions here, you will end up on the winning side of the battle for souls. You will see your life count while you are young!

Starting a R.I.O.T. (and reaching people for Jesus) is not boring. In fact, it can be an adventure of a lifetime. It is like joining a band of revolutionaries out to change the world. More fun than you could imagine and more of a rush than anything you have ever done, helping people find heaven is a blast.

So fasten your seat belts and hang on tight! You are in for the ride of your life as you gather friends around you and start a R.I.O.T. There is no time to wait. Get some friends to read through this manual with you and start planning your R.I.O.T. today!

Part 1
THE BRIEFING ROOM

1. WHAT IS A R.I.O.T.?

It was a load of dynamite waiting to explode. The whole country waited with anticipation for the jury to decide. Someone would be disappointed no matter what the final decision was. As the verdict for the police officers accused of beating Rodney King came sweeping across the air waves—*not guilty*—the unthinkable happened in downtown Los Angeles: a riot!

It all started one night when King decided to drink and drive. He was going 80 mph when a highway patrol officer tried to pull him over. King knew if he were caught he would be sent back to prison for violating parole, so he ran. For eight miles, he tried to outrun the police cars that chased him. When finally cornered, King responded slowly or not at all to the police officers' orders, and even two hits with their stun guns seemed to have no effect on him.

When King, an African-American, fought off the officers

trying to handcuff him and ran, the four white officers tried to subdue him by more violent means. At this point, a guy across the street began to capture the scene on video.

King was arrested and brought to trial, but many Americans had seen and knew no more details than the beating of an African-American man by four white police officers. Many were outraged and vowed revenge. When the trial resulted in an innocent verdict for the police officers, Los Angeles went wild.

Crowds ran down streets looting stores and breaking windows. People of every race hit, stabbed and beat anyone who got in their way. Rioters pulled drivers from their cars, then tipped over the cars and burned them. The victims were people of every age and race. Some lost their life savings as their businesses burned to the ground. Others lost their lives.

The National Guard was called in, but it took a long time to quiet the anarchy. By the time things settled down, more than 50 people were dead, 2,300 injured and over $1 billion in property damage done. Like it or not, what many never thought could happen in the United States had happened: A RIOT!

Webster's dictionary defines *riot* as an *unrestrained uproar in a public place.*[1] What happened in L.A. certainly was an unrestrained uproar in a public place. Let's look a little closer and check out what that really means.

First of all, a riot is "unrestrained." You can try all you want—as the police in L.A. did—but you cannot control it. The fury is so great, the passion so deep, that there is no restraining it. There are no rules—rioters make their own rules. A riot is like a wildfire in the forest that cannot be contained. Get out of the way, or be blown out of its way.

A riot is an "uproar." It is like an explosion. In fact, the purpose of a riot is to get noticed. The louder the uproar, the more it will be noticed. Like an earthquake to the people who are watching the riot from afar, it lets them know the seriousness of the matter.

Notice that a riot does not take place in private. It is out in

---

1 *Webster's Tenth New Collegiate Dictionary,* Merriam-Webster, 1993.

the open where everybody can see it. By its nature, it cannot be private. It has to get people's attention. Those in the riot are not ashamed that others are watching; they are proud. They will get their message out no matter what the cost. They feel they have tried everything they know and no one has listened. They feel forced to do something in a big, very visible way.

PAUL'S BAD HABIT

These men who have caused trouble all over the world have now come here. (Acts 17:6)

That's what the city officials in Thessalonica said about Paul. That was his reputation. Everywhere he went, Paul stirred things up. In the King James Version, Acts 17:6 says, "These that have *turned the world upside down* are come hither also."

This was the accusation brought against Paul when he

preached the gospel. Take a moment and read for yourself the whole story:

> . . . They came to Thessalonica, where there was a Jewish synagogue. As his custom was, Paul went into the synagogue, and on three Sabbath days he reasoned with them from the Scriptures, explaining and proving that the Christ had to suffer and rise from the dead. "This Jesus I am proclaiming to you is the Christ," he said. Some of the Jews were persuaded and joined Paul and Silas, as did a large number of God-fearing Greeks and not a few prominent women.

> But the Jews were jealous; so they rounded up some bad characters from the marketplace, formed a mob and started a riot in the city. They rushed to Jason's house in search of Paul and Silas in order to bring them out to the crowd. But when they did not find them, they dragged Jason and some other brothers before the city officials, shouting: "These

men who have caused trouble all over the world have now come here." (Acts 17:1–6)

Paul did what God called him to do—preach and help people get their lives together with the power of God—and everyone got upset about it. The devil gets mad when you threaten his territory, but Paul didn't care. He kept pressing on. One time, he even said, "Woe to me if I do not preach the gospel!" (1 Cor. 9:16). In other words, *I've got to preach! This thing will eat me alive if I don't!*

As you read through the book of Acts, you can see that almost everywhere Paul went he was met with outrage. Some people traveled great distances just to incite the crowds against him. Paul met so much resistance because when people have an encounter with the living God, they are forced to repent or riot.

While preaching in Lystra, Paul was dragged out of town by an angry mob, stoned and left for dead. His disciples came and prayed for him, then he went back into the *same city* to preach again (see Acts 14:19–20)! In Jerusalem, he had a whole crowd screaming at him, lifting him over their heads, ready to kill him. When the authorities rescued him, he asked if he could speak to the crowd for a few minutes. This guy had guts! He was like the Energizer Bunny: he just kept going and going and going . . . (read Acts 21-22 for all the details).

Paul had a reputation for stirring things up. What's your reputation? Sometimes we worry so much about ruffling people's feathers that we do not do what God has called us to do. We worry more about what other people think of us than what God thinks of us.

> . . . A R.I.O.T IS LIKE AN UNRESTRAINED
> UPROAR IN A PUBLIC PLACE, TURBULENT,
> RIGHT IN
>
> YOUR FACE WITH THE FACTS, WE'RE GONNA
> SPREAD
>
> GOD'S WORD AND ATTACK EVERY LIE YOU'VE
> HEARD

LIKE THE DOCTRINES OF MEN THAT ARE
STILL

FALLEN PREY TO THE SILVERY SWORD OF
GOD'S WORD TODAY.[2]

It's Time for a 20th-Century Holy Riot!

Righteous: Acting in accord with divine or moral law; free from guilt or sin. Arising from an outraged sense of justice or morality. To conform to the Bible.

Invasion: Military aggression. Incursion of an army for conquest or plunder. An armed attack.

Of Truth: Loyalty or faithfulness to a standard. Reality. The real state of affairs.[3]

---

2 Lyrics from "R.I.O.T" by Carman. © 1995 Some-O-Dat Music (admin. by Word, Inc.) (BMI) / Bases Loaded Music Sierra Sky Songs (Bases Loaded Music and Sierra Sky Songs admin. by EMI Christian Music Publishing) (ASCAP) All rights reserved. Used by permission.

3 *Webster's Tenth New Collegiate Dictionary,* Merriam-Webster, 1993.

A Righteous Invasion of Truth is what we need. It is time for us to develop the same attitude Paul had, the attitude that compelled him to change the world.

In a Righteous Invasion of Truth (R.I.O.T.), rather than being destroyed, people's lives are put back together. There may be some wreckage, though. When Satan's plans are destroyed he gets stinking mad. But we say it's about time we made him mad!

In a R.I.O.T., God comes on the scene and people are never the same again. It is time for us to throw off our restraints and go for it. Start ruffling some feathers; stop being so polite to the devil! Quit playing it safe and step out on the edge for God. He is looking for someone with guts enough to go for it! A R.I.O.T. is a risk-taking operation. You don't risk your life, as they did in the L.A. riots; you risk your reputation.

A R.I.O.T. is young people taking their faith seriously and doing something about what they believe. Take the gospel to the public places and let this world know that Jesus is alive. Let people know that Jesus is alive in *you*! It takes no courage to be a Christian in private. It is when you break out into the open that people notice you. That is what a R.I.O.T. is all about—doing things in public to let the world know that Jesus is alive.

There are already a lot of young people stirring things up in the devil's domain. Over one million teens participate in "See You at the Pole" events every September. The "True Love Waits" campaign for moral purity has received commitments from about 200,000 teens. The number of missions organizations for teenagers has grown phenomenally over the last few years. And there are about 14,000 student-led Bible Clubs on high school campuses across America. These are things *teenagers* are doing. These are things *you* could be doing!

A R.I.O.T. is using every spare moment to reach out to lost people. It is creatively expanding the kingdom of God. It is strategizing and coordinating with friends to take over a part of your school or town for Jesus. It is a full-blown blitz! It is making everyone think, *God, God, God! That is all I ever see and hear! God stuff is everywhere!*

That's right! That is exactly what we want them to think. We say, "Get the picture, dude! God's got your number. He is after you!"

GET A VISION FOR A R.I.O.T.

This manual is designed to help you start a R.I.O.T.—a Righteous Invasion of Truth—in your personal life, your school, your work and everywhere else you live. We do not want you to just read about it—we want you involved in a R.I.O.T. Reading this manual *and doing what it says* will be your first step toward the adventure of a lifetime.

Why not start a R.I.O.T. right where you are? This manual will give you all the tools and ideas you need. You can start by yourself, with some friends or with your youth group; but whatever you do, *start!* It'll be a rippin' blast. This is your chance to be like Paul. Earn yourself a reputation as someone who turns the world upside down everywhere you go.

One thing we can promise you is *you won't get bored!* In this R.I.O.T. Manual, you'll find so many great ideas that by the time you finish you may want to start all over again. Or maybe you'll want to think up your own ideas.

James, a junior in high school, was a fairly new Christian. But he had an intensity about the Lord and he shared his faith freely with friends at school. One day, two of the players on the high school football team got into trouble with their parents and were grounded. Desperate to get out of the house, they asked their parents if they could go to a Bible study. Their parents agreed. The guys didn't know of any Bible studies, but they knew James. They asked him if he would lead a Bible study for a few of them. James was surprised, until the guys explained it was the only way they could get out of the house. James agreed to do the Bible study anyway.

James got prayed up and made sure he was ready for God to move through him to reach these guys. About thirty football players and their friends showed up the first night. As James shared his passion for Christ, these guys who had come for fun began to listen. When James finished speaking, every person there was on his face, weeping and committing his life to God.

As word of the Bible study spread over the next few weeks, many more came. By the end of the year, more than three hundred teenagers had visited or were coming to the Bible study on a weekly basis. It took only one committed believer—James—to start a R.I.O.T. in that town.

God can use you, too, to affect where you live, to change the way people see God and to change where they will spend eternity. Don't you agree that *it is time to start a Righteous Invasion of Truth?!!*

2. WHY START A R.I.O.T?

A riot usually starts when people are dissatisfied with the status quo. Tired of putting up with too much for too long, they say it is time for a change.

Scripture says, "From the days of John the Baptist until

now, the kingdom of heaven has been forcefully **advancing,** and forceful men lay hold of it" (Matt. 11:12). Jesus tells us here that He came to change the status quo. He points out that since He and John came on the scene, some amazing things had happened in God's kingdom. After years of relative quiet, someone showed up who knew what was supposed to happen and by force took hold of God's kingdom.

Today, God is looking for some young people to do the same, people who have had enough of the world cramming sin and a sinful lifestyle down their throats and acting like it is cool. Since the Garden of Eden, the devil has had a free-for-all —abusing, taking advantage of and deceiving people— with almost no resistance. He has manipulated us and given us a raw deal for so long that we accept it as the way things are supposed to be. We think it is normal to be ripped off by Satan. It happens all the time, but we don't get mad because *we're used to it.*

Well, we think it's time to get mad—mad enough to start a R.I.O.T.

LIKE A CHURCH ON THE MOVE THAT WILL NOT
    DOUBLE BACK

FROM THE FIGHT, 'CAUSE WE'RE SALT AND
    LIGHT

AND WE THRIVE ON JESUS, THE THEME OF
    OUR LIVES

AND HERE'S THE SPIN—LOVE NOTHIN' BUT
    GOD, HATE NOTHIN' BUT SIN.[4]

WHY WE SHOULD BE MAD

Before the L.A. riot, racial tensions mounted for a long time. People felt abused, taken advantage of and deceived. They felt they always got the raw end of the deal. Finally, they were pushed over the edge to DO something about it. The Rodney King trial verdict was the motivation they needed to revolt. A riot was the natural result.

It's time for us to be mad that young people sit mesmer-

---

4 Lryics from "R.I.0.T" by Carman.

ized for hours by mind-numbing music videos, distracted from paying attention to eternal issues. We should get mad that teens listen to hours and hours of anti-God, anti-Jesus music every day and spend only a few minutes reading the Bible (if that much!). We ought to be infuriated that many young people find their purpose for life in sports rather than in the One who made them in the first place.

Likewise, we should be sick and tired of all the *safe-sex* jargon and of school officials who pass out condoms and advocate homosexuality as a normal, alternative lifestyle. The fact that 6,000 teens kill themselves every year ought to make us mad. We ought to be ticked off that teenage drunk driving is the second biggest killer of young people today. In addition, hearing statistics of the huge numbers of teens into drugs should make us want to do something about it. The fact that 1.2 million babies are born each year to unwed teens ought to drive us to action.[5]

Are you sick of hearing about this stuff? Are you tired of

---

5 *Tulsa World,* June 7, 1995, p. 5.

the bad stuff getting all the publicity? Are you mad enough to do something about it? Then it's time for us to get some of our own publicity! Instead of complaining about how bad things are, let's DO SOMETHING TO CHANGE THINGS! It is time to start a R.I.O.T.!

Take a few minutes and list some things the devil has done in your school, work or community that make you mad:

1. _____

2. _____

3. _____

Are you mad enough at the devil to do something about it? Do you love God enough to change things? It's time to quit being passive. No more Mr. or Ms. Nice Guy. It's time for a R.I.O.T.

WHAT WE DON'T NEED

We don't need another retreat; we need a R.I.O.T.!

We don't need a little revival; we need a R.I.O.T.!

We don't need a pizza party; we need a R.I.O.T.!

We don't need watered-down, candy-coated, ear-tickling verbiage; we need a R.I.O.T.!

We don't need more Christian activities; we need a R.I.O.T.!

We don't need a bunch of young people who look spiritual on the outside but in their hearts are far away from God; we need a R.I.O.T.!

Got the picture yet? Maybe not . . .

We don't need more Christian ball teams; we need a R.I.O.T.!

We don't need more Christian T-shirts and paraphernalia; we need a R.I.O.T.!

We don't need more sermons that we forget next week; WE NEED A R.I.O.T.!

IT'S TRUE, WE LOOK TO HEAVEN AND OUR
    MANSIONS IN THE SKY
IT'S TRUE, WE'VE GOT THE GAZE OF ETERNITY
    IN OUR EYES
BEFORE THIS CHURCH IS RAPTURED
THERE'S NO WAY WE'RE GONNA LEAVE HERE
    QUIET
WE WANT A RIGHTEOUS INVASION OF TRUTH
WE WANT A R.I.O.T.[6]

---

6 Lyrics from "R.I.O.T." by Carman.

WHAT ARE THE RESULTS OF A R.I.O.T.?

A holy R.I.O.T. should bring about real change in people's lives. Reservations should be made in heaven. The way people live ought to be different. After a R.I.O.T. has been through our communities, there should be more people in our youth groups and churches.

When you bring a R.I.O.T. to town, the locals should know that you have been there. The city council and mayor should know that you are doing something to stir up righteousness in your town. The newspapers and T.V. stations should know that something is going on with your R.I.O.T. Squad. When you start a R.I.O.T., everyone will know.

A R.I.O.T. STARTS IN YOU

A R.I.O.T. is not something you do; it is something that results from who you are. It is not a bunch of crazy Christian activities designed to irritate people. It is your heart beating with love for the people around you. It all begins with a Righteous Invasion of Truth in your own life. You then take your walk with God seriously and go after Him with all your heart. You get your roots deep into Jesus so you can give an answer when people ask you about the hope that you have (see 1 Pet. 3:15).

You experience a radical change of your heart for God. You realize that to love Him is to love the people He died to save. Your heart has been so completely turned on and you are so alive in Him, that you can't wait for others to hear! A R.I.O.T. beats in your heart long before you actually do anything to start one. A R.I.O.T. happens when you cannot stand the thought of one more person going to hell.

Take some time right now and ask God to start a R.I.O.T. in your heart. Get into the Word and see what it says about God's heart for people and the incredible compassion He has for them. Eat up those Scriptures until they become ALIVE to you. That is where the R.I.O.T. starts—in the heart of a radical believer willing to live on the edge!

Let's stop talking about changing the world; let's start a R.I.O.T.!

JESUS, WE'RE CALLIN' ON YOUR NAME

JESUS, WE'RE GONNA SEE A CHANGE

JESUS, WE'RE TAKIN' ON GOLIATH

WITH A RIGHTEOUS INVASION OF TRUTH

WE WANT A R.I.O.T. [7]

3. FORMING A R.I.O.T. SQUAD

So we all agree we need a R.I.O.T. The question is how do you start one? Well, you don't do it alone. You need a R.I.O.T. Squad to help you. A R.I.O.T. Squad is a group of wild teens who want to stir up some trouble for the devil. They are tired of living a boring Christian life and they want some action. They don't *talk* about doing something; they actually go for it. And they need each other to pull it off.

Sometimes God will encourage you to do things on your

---

7 Lyrics from "R.I.O.T" by Carman.

own, and you need to act on those things. However, God doesn't call us to be Lone Ranger Christians. Scripture says, "Let us consider how we may spur one another on toward love and good deeds. Let us not give up meeting together . . ." (Heb. 10:24-25). Get hooked up with other people who have the same passion and fire for God that you have.

Look at the example of Paul. He never did things alone; he always had Barnabas, Silas, Timothy or a whole group of people with him. They blasted into a new village with the Gospel and wild things broke out. They stood together in persecution and high-fived each other when a whole town got saved! Can you imagine the great conversations they might have had between villages:

> *Wasn't that cool how all those people got healed back there? I wonder what will happen at the next place. Last time we were thrown in jail, and the time before we were beaten up for the Gospel. Wow, are we having good times here or what?!!*

Why not follow Paul's example and put together a R.I.O.T. Squad of your own? You can start with as few as two people in your Squad, but try to get at least four. Then you can build it to as many as you want. It is great to do things for the Lord by yourself, but when you gather together a handful of other blazing fanatics to pull off a R.I.O.T., it becomes a lot more fun and effective.

ENLISTING SQUAD MEMBERS

Begin by approaching one at a time a few teens you think are willing to go for it. Ask them if they are interested in having the adventure of a lifetime. Get a commitment from them to stick with the R.I.O.T. Squad at least until Carman tours your area (see R.I.O.T. tour dates in the back of this manual). Once you have three or four other teens into it, set a time, date and place to get together.

List three or four people who you think would be great R.I.O.T. Squad members:

1. _____

2. _____

3. _____

4. _____

Now, start talking to them about it today!

During your first official R.I.O.T. Squad meeting, give members a vision of what you will be doing. Remember, you want them into it as much as you are, so let them have input. Don't make it "my Squad," but "our Squad."

Your first time together you will want to:

- Come up with names of others who may want to join your R.I.O.T. Squad.

- Make sure everyone gets a copy of this R.I.O.T. Manual. All Squad members should read it and understand the vision for a R.I.O.T.

- Talk about what R.I.O.T. gear you will need.

- Look at all the R.I.O.T. tactics listed in Part 3 and decide which ones you will tackle first.

- Decide when to start implementing the tactics.

- Set a date for your next meeting.

HINT: One of the things you can do to get your R.I.O.T. Squad pumped up is attend an Acquire The Fire Youth Convention when it comes to your area. Acquire The Fire can help you: 1) get your R.I.O.T. Squad focused, tight and ready for action; and 2) find others who want to start a R.I.O.T. Squad. Call 1–800–329–FIRE for information on the Acquire The Fire nearest you.

HOW TO START A R.I.O.T.

A R.I.O.T. starts when a R.I.O.T. Squad takes action. You can plan an invasion of your school or community, strategizing a whole month's worth of tactics at one meeting. You are the revolutionaries—it is up to you when you start a R.I.O.T. in your area. Remember, there are no rules in a R.I.O.T. except:

- Obey the Bible

- Honor your authorities

- Establish your own operating procedures as you go.

Remember the unrestrained uproar we talked about earlier? Now is the time to let it kick in! Are you mad about what the devil has been doing? Now is the time to do something about it!

INVOLVE YOUR YOUTH GROUP

This is a perfect opportunity for your youth group to reach out to others. Take this manual and what you have learned from it and ask your pastor to pull the youth group together into a R.I.O.T. Squad.

YOUTH PASTORS: A R.I.O.T. is a fresh approach to get your kids to do something for God, without some of the old stigma of a "street witnessing team." You do not have to get your whole youth group to participate. Just pull together those who really want to go for it. After a while the others will see their excitement and want to join in on the fun. This is a chance to put a new twist on evangelism and let the kids do some of the planning themselves. If you already have an outreach program, you can incorporate the concept and ideas of a R.I.O.T. Squad into it. A R.I.O.T. Squad can supplement what you are doing now and make it easy for you to get your kids involved in ministry.

THE GOAL OF A R.I.O.T. SQUAD

God is not interested in seeing a little skirmish or a bunch of Christian activities. He is honored most by *lasting* results. We want to see God show up on the scene and minister to people through your R.I.O.T. Squad. We want to see lives changed and people saved! Keeping all this in mind, be aggressive as you plan your tactics. Don't use one now and then; keep a whole bunch of them going at once. Come on! We need a R.I.O.T., not a flurry!

Don't measure your success by how many souls you save; leave that to the Lord. Set your goals in terms of how many tactics you implement (see Weapons and Tactics Checklist, p. 140-41). The minimum goal for each R.I.O.T. Squad is to implement three weapons and three tactics for each R.I.O.T. Zone. That's twenty-seven weapons and twenty-seven tactics put into action. Just imagine what you can do to destroy the devil's plans with that many tactics!

Take some time right now and plan your first R.I.O.T. Squad meeting. Set the date and time. Call and invite your potential Squad members. Pray your face off. You are about to change the world with a R.I.O.T.!

PART 2
WEAPONS

We Christians are in a war, but our war is not against the devil. Jesus won that war when He died on the cross. We battle for the souls of people. We fight to keep our faith alive and to share it with others (see 1 Tim. 1:18).

God has not put us in the middle of a war without giving us weapons. If your R.I.O.T. is going to have lasting results, you'd better know what weapons you have and how to use them strategically. Some of the weapons that the Lord has given us we use to defend ourselves against the devil. God knows that the devil will try to attack you, especially as you begin a R.I.O.T., so He provides protection. These defensive weapons keep you from getting picked off by Satan and his buddies. They help you defend yourself against "all the flaming arrows of the evil one" (Eph. 6:16).

But God wants us to do more than defend the territory we already have; He wants us to take over enemy territory! To do that, we have to advance into areas where the devil now dominates. The Bible says:

> *For our struggle is not against flesh and blood,*
> *but against the rulers, against the authorities,*
> *against the powers of this dark world and*
> *against the spiritual forces of evil in the heav-*
> *enly realms.* (Eph. 6:12)

Our R.I.O.T. is spiritual, so we'd better know how to use spiritual weapons before we go into war.

ARE YOU PREPARED FOR A R.I.O.T.?

> *Put on the full armor of God so that you can*
> *take your stand against the devil's schemes.*
> (Eph. 6:11)

When you start a R.I.O.T., you are messing with the devil's territory. That's why Paul says to put on the FULL ARMOR. Don't try to fight the devil half-naked! Let's look at the weapons God has provided for you to start a R.I.O.T. Before it is over you will use every one of them.

1. BULLETPROOF VEST

Police officers never know when someone might take a shot at them. They must be prepared at all times. Their bulletproof vests keep them safe from bullets flying in their direction. The vest protects the police officers' most vulnerable areas. If shot in the arm or leg an officer won't die on the spot, but if hit in the heart it's all over.

R.I.O.T. Squad members need protection for their weak areas too. Look at the areas of your life where you have been weak in the past, and strengthen those areas. Don't go into a R.I.O.T. *hoping* you are strong enough not to fall into past mistakes. Instead, double up your protection in those areas.

How do you do it? We're glad you asked!

First, in every area where you have been weak in the past, **build yourself up in the Word of God.** If you have had a problem losing your temper, find Scriptures dealing with anger. For example,

> *In your anger do not sin: Do not let the sun go down while you are still angry.* (Eph. 4:26)

If you have a problem with saying bad things about people, meditate on this verse:

> *Do not let any unwholesome talk come out of your mouths, but only what is helpful for building others up according to their needs, that it may benefit those who listen.* (Eph. 4:29)

Find verses like these and memorize them. Write them on index cards and carry them with you everywhere you go.

While trying to reach people for Jesus in a R.I.O.T., you do not want your temper to blow up or your mouth to shoot off. So build up yourself in every vulnerable area so the devil can't hit you where it hurts.

Another way to protect yourself is by having *accountabil-*

ity friends. Let a few other people—fellow R.I.O.T. Squad members, maybe—know the areas where you feel weak so they can encourage you. Ask them to stay *in your face* about those areas. Ask them to keep pushing you to get stronger, and to help you see areas in your life that are still weak. It is better for a friend to see your weak areas and tell you, than for the devil to see them and tempt you. The Bible says, "Wounds from a friend can be trusted, but an enemy multiplies kisses" (Prov. 27:6). This means that accountability friends can be trusted—even if they tell you something you do not want to hear. They look out for you and help you strengthen your weak areas. So when you start a R.I.O.T., be sure to wear your bulletproof vest by building yourself up in the Word and by having some accountability friends.

2. CONCEALED WEAPONS

Also available to you are concealed weapons. Although lethal, most people never know you are carrying them. Here are your concealed weapons:

1. Holy Spirit. Here's what Jesus said about the Holy Spirit: *The world cannot accept him, because it neither sees him nor knows him. But you know him, for he lives with you and will be in you.* (John 14:17)

There are gun detectors and metal detectors installed in many high schools today, but they don't have any Holy Ghost detectors yet! What are they going to do — send you home if you bring the Holy Spirit to school? Nah! Kids say, "We can't pray at school!" Who is there to stop you? They say you cannot bring God into the school. You cannot help but bring Him in; He lives inside you!

2. Pocket Bible. Take a Bible with you wherever you go; don't leave home without it. It doesn't have to be huge; a small one is all you need. Read it when you have a few minutes between classes. Refer to it all day long. Use it to help people who are struggling.

As a R.I.O.T. Squad member, you are totally into God. You want His Word with you wherever you are. Have it handy so you can regularly blast your brain with it!

3. R.I.O.T. Manual. We made it small so you could carry it all the time. Refer to it for ideas on how to keep a R.I.O.T. going. Use it to remind yourself of the tactics you commit to and the weapons you have. Carry it so you will remember specific tools for sharing your faith. The Bible is your Sword; the R.I.O.T. Manual is your dagger.

4. Memorized Scripture. This concealed weapon is powerful. Learn Scriptures that will minister to people. Be able to use the Bible to show others how to give their lives to the Lord. Store Scriptures like these in your heart:

> *For God so loved the world that he gave his one and only Son, that whoever believes in him shall not perish but have eternal life.* (John 3:16)
>
> *For all have sinned and fall short of the glory of God.* (Rom. 3:23)

For the wages of sin is death, but the gift of God is eternal life in Christ Jesus our Lord. (Rom. 6:23)

But what does it say? "The word is near you; it is in your mouth and in your heart," that is, the word of faith we are proclaiming. (Rom. 10:8)

If you confess with your mouth, "Jesus is Lord," and believe in your heart that God raised him from the dead, you will be saved. For it is with your heart that you believe and are justified, and it is with your mouth that you confess and are saved. (Rom. 10:9–10)

Come to me, all you who are weary and burdened, and I will give you rest. Take my yoke upon you and learn from me, for I am gentle and humble in heart, and you will find rest for your souls. For my yoke is easy and my burden is light. (Matt. 11:28–30)

Here I am! I stand at the door and knock. If anyone hears my voice and opens the door, I will come in and eat with him, and he with me. (Rev. 3:20)

Learn these Scriptures backwards and forwards. Hide them in your heart, so you can use them whenever you need them.

3. I.D.

What does it mean to I.D. yourself? You know who you are in Christ. You are confident that He has done in you what He said He would. You don't have to be looking over your shoulder wondering if He is really with you. With this weapon, you can stand strong and confident in the middle of your R.I.O.T.

I HAVE BEEN BOUGHT WITH A PRICE WHEN
    JESUS HUNG ON A TREE

MY LIFE IS NOT MY OWN, I'LL NEVER FOLLOW
    YOUR LEAD

YOU BUILD UP ALL THE PLEASURE OF SIN IN
    PEOPLE'S EYES

BUT NEVER TELL THE CONSEQUENCES OF THE
    COMPROMISE

YOU USED TO HAVE MY NUMBER, BUT THIS
    TIME YOU WILL FAIL

SO GET THEE BEHIND ME, SATAN, I'M NOT FOR
    SALE [8]

In the middle of a R.I.O.T., you'll need to know what God thinks of you. Fill your brain with Scriptures like these:

I can do everything through him who gives me strength. (Phil. 4:13)

In all these things we are more than conquerors through him who loved us. (Rom. 8:37)

For I am convinced that neither death nor life, neither angels nor demons, neither the present nor the future, nor any powers, neither height nor depth, nor anything else in all creation, will be able to separate us from the love of God that is in Christ Jesus our Lord. (Rom. 8:38–39)

You, dear children, are from God and have overcome them, because the one who is in you is greater than the one who is in the world. (1 John 4:4)

And surely I will be with you always, to the very end of the age. (Matt. 28:20)

Get these verses burning down inside you, so you know without a doubt who you are and that God backs you up. Then you'll realize there is nothing that can stop you!

4. SWORD OF THE SPIRIT

The word of God is living and active. Sharper than any double-edged sword, it penetrates even to dividing soul and spirit, joints and marrow; it judges the thoughts and attitudes of the heart. (Heb. 4:12)

The Bible in your hand may look like any other book, but it is *living and active*. It is alive. Know how to use it to help people understand the Lord. Don't cut them up with your sword as some have done; build them up. Most people know they have blown it before you tell them. You don't have to make them feel worse by using Scripture. Remember, the Gospel is *good* news. Present it in the right way, using

Scriptures that show the benefits of loving God, and watch what happens. Here are some examples of Scriptures to use:

> But seek first his kingdom and his righteousness, and all these things will be given to you as well. (Matt. 6:33)

> [God] redeems your life from the pit and crowns you with love and compassion. (Ps. 103:4)

> My God will meet all your needs according to his glorious riches in Christ Jesus. (Phil. 4:19)

> Whatever you have learned or received or heard from me, or seen in me—put it into practice. And the God of peace will be with you. (Phil. 4:9)

> Come to me, all you who are weary and burdened, and I will give you rest. (Matt. 11:28)

He himself bore our sins in his body on the tree, so that we might die to sins and live for righteousness; by his wounds you have been healed.
(1 Pet. 2:24)

These are all examples of how you can use the Sword of the Spirit to build up people. It is God who puts us back together again. He blesses us and meets all our needs. He gives us peace like nothing the world can give. He makes the weak strong. He heals the sick. He is what this world is looking for, they just don't know it. So use the Bible to help people know that God is on their side.

5. Cuffs

Use your cuffs to bind the devil. It does no good to go in where the devil is running around and start trying to do something for God. You have to take charge of the situation as Jesus described:

No one can enter a strong man's house and carry off his possessions unless he first ties up the strong man. Then he can rob his house. (Mark 3:27)

If we are going to start a Righteous Invasion of Truth, we first have to bind the devil. We take authority over him and let him know we will no longer tolerate what he is doing. Jesus said:

*And these signs will accompany those who believe: In my name **they will drive out demons**; they will speak in new tongues; they will pick up snakes with their hands; and when they drink deadly poison, it will not hurt them at all; they will place their hands on sick people, and they will get well.* (Mark 16:17-18, emphasis added)

How do you cuff 'em? How do you bind the devil and drive out demons? Simply say something like this:

> *Devil, in Jesus' name, I come against you and bind you away from my school and my work. Take your hands off my friends, (name them), and take the blinders off their eyes. I refuse to let you run this place any more. By the power of the Holy Spirit, I rebuke you and tell you to let them **go**! Jesus gave me authority over you, so you must get out!*

It is clear that we are supposed to take charge of the spiritual realm. If this is where our struggle is, then this is where we'd better fight. Don't start any tactic in your R.I.O.T. without first binding the devil.

6. TESTIMONY

*They overcame him by the blood of the Lamb,
and by the word of their testimony.* (Rev. 12:11)

This weapon is your own story or testimony. If you think
there isn't much value to telling your own story, you don't
understand what a testimony is. The dictionary calls a testimony "a firsthand authentication of fact."[9] Your testimony is
the story of what God has done in your life, not some made-
up story that you found in a book. The good news is we all
have our own story.

Think about what was going on in your mind and heart
before you knew Jesus. Think about how lonely or confused
you were or how you really needed a friend. Maybe you
were messed up on drugs. Or maybe you were just a regular
sinner like the rest of the world. Either way, you have a story.

If you were saved when you were young, you may think,
I don't have a real testimony. I've been saved most of my life.

---

9 *Webster's Tenth New Collegiate Dictionary*, Merriam-Webster, 1993.

That is probably the best testimony there is! That is what God wants for everyone. You have not been messed up by the world's system. You have been protected from a world of heartache. If you think, *I can't relate to the world,* then thank God you can't! Show them what life could be like. Show them that this thing works!

Your testimony is more than what happened the day you were saved. It is an account of what God has done in your life since then. It is "telling the truth about God." Talk about the last time He answered an urgent prayer request. Or the way He healed you or gave you peace in the middle of a confusing time in your life.

People can argue with you about what the Scriptures mean. They can argue about what you think is true. *But they can never argue with what you have experienced.* The Bible says that is how we overcome—by Jesus' blood and by talking about what God has done in our lives.

Take some time now and think through what God has done in your life this year. Write out your testimony here. It doesn't have to be long, but it does need to be clear. Then the next time someone asks you, "How do you know this thing is real?," you can tell all the incredible things that God has done in your life.

MY TESTIMONY

_____

_____

_____

_____

_____

_____

_____

7. HEART OF COMPASSION

When he saw the crowds, he had compassion on them, because they were harassed and helpless, like sheep without a shepherd. (Matt. 9:36)

Jesus could not look at a crowd without having compassion on them. He knew how much God loved them and was *moved* with compassion. As you prepare for a R.I.O.T., one of your biggest needs is a heart full of compassion for the people you are about to reach. Some people have warm fuzzy feelings but never do anything about those feelings. They think they feel compassion but what they really feel is sympathy. If it were Jesus' kind of compassion, they would do something about it.

Other people want to do a lot of things for God to reach people, but they have no compassion. They are motivated by guilt or a desire to earn something from God. They think that God will like them better if they reach those poor people. *No way!* You cannot do anything to get God to love you more. He already loves you to the fullest extent.

The only reason to reach out to others is in response to God's love. We get so blown away by His love for us that we want others to know it, too. People can tell whether or not you are motivated by love. They can tell if you really care about them or your own interests. If you minister to them for the fun you get out of it or to make yourself look good, your ministry will be ineffective.

Pray now and ask God to break your heart for the lost people around you. Ask Him to let you see them the way He sees them. Ask Him for the same compassion that Jesus felt when He saw people as sheep without a shepherd. Stay on your knees until you feel God's heart of love welling up inside you. Don't stop praying until God's compassion for people has overwhelmed you. A heart of compassion will *help you endure* and will *help you break through to people's hearts* when they sense God's love in you.

8. WORSHIP

Starting a R.I.O.T. that will make a difference requires God's presence right there with you. Don't be out in enemy territory alone. You want God to show up and silence every mocker. You want Him to blow people away with His power.

If you want God to show up on the scene like that, He must be in your life that way. It's not abracadabra and *poof*, there He is! Make sure He is blowing you away with His presence every day so you don't have to conjure Him up in the midst of a R.I.O.T.

The best way for you to get into God's presence is to worship Him like crazy. Here's how:

Enter his gates with thanksgiving and his courts with praise; give thanks to him and praise his name. (Ps. 100:4)

To get into the courts of the Lord, begin thanking and praising Him. Keep hanging out in His courts to be around Him and get His presence rubbing off on you.

The song "7 Ways 2 Praise" from Carman's R.I.O.T. album details ways that the children of Israel learned to worship the Lord. It's a good idea to experience them yourself before you implement your R.I.O.T. Tactics.

NUMBER ONE IS TOWDAH IT'S THE SACRIFICE

PRAISING GOD IN SPITE THE FACT YOUR WORLD IS IN A VICE

IT'S PRAISE THAT PUSHES THROUGH THE WALL OF ALL ADVERSITY

AN OFFERING THAT FLOWS TO HEAVEN IN OUR TIME OF NEED [10]

As you get ready to start a R.I.O.T. in your town, you may see a lot of garbage going on around you. Praise God anyway. He is bigger than all that stuff. Push through and really worship Him. Not because you feel like it, but because He is worth it. Thank Him in the middle of your need. Why? Because He promised to meet all of your needs, so your answer is on the way.

NUMBER TWO'S YADAH THAT MEANS TO LIFT YOUR HANDS

IN RESPONSE TO WHAT THE LORD HAS DONE THROUGHOUT THE LAND [11]

---

10 Lyrics from "7 Ways 2 Praise" by Carman. © 1995 Some-O-Dat Music (admin. by Word, Inc.) (BMI)/Bases Loaded Music/Sierra Sky Songs (Bases Loaded Music and Sierra Sky Songs admin. by EMI Christian Music Publishing) (ASCAP) All rights reserved. Used by permission.

11 Lyrics from "7 Ways 2 Praise" by Carman.

Think through all God has done in your life and thank Him for it all. Sometimes we pray, and when the answer comes we forget to say thank you. Think about what God is doing in your family and at your school, then thank Him. If you already have started your R.I.O.T. Squad, think about what He is doing through you. Let Him know you appreciate what He has done.

> NUMBER THREE IS BAROUCH THAT SIMPLY MEANS TO BOW
>
> IN THE AWESOME PRESENCE OF THE LORD AND ALL HIS POWER
>
> TO JUST BE OVERWHELMED 'CAUSE YOU HARDLY CAN BELIEVE
>
> THAT YOU'VE BEEN GIVEN FAVOR BY HIS HOLY MAJESTY [12]

---

12 Lyrics from "7 Ways 2 Praise" by Carman.

Now you are in the inner sanctuary. It is time to get on your face before the Lord and honor Him. Realize who He is and who you are. He is God Almighty who made this whole world! Get close to God's throne and do what comes naturally when you get there. Every time the Bible records a worship service in heaven, they are all on their knees:

> *Whenever the living creatures give glory, honor and thanks to him who sits on the throne and who lives for ever and ever, the twenty-four elders **fall down before him** who sits on the throne, and worship him who lives for ever and ever. They lay their crowns before the throne and say: "You are worthy, our Lord and God, to receive glory and honor and power, for you created all things, and by your will they were created and have their being." (Rev. 4:9-11, emphasis added)*

Now is the time to get in the presence of the Lord—not while you are in a R.I.O.T. If you want the presence of the Lord to go with you, start by getting on your knees now to worship Him. There is no better weapon for a R.I.O.T. than to have God blow people away with His own presence.

PART 3
TACTICS

Tactics of war are how actual strategy unfolds. This is where all the talk stops and the action begins. It is also where the fun begins. You are about to launch an invasion of the most holy kind. You are about to march into enemy territory and take it back.

You will join the ranks of others who already have stepped out on the edge to do something for God—and in the process, changed their world. You will keep company with people like the apostle Paul who marched from town to town stirring things up for God. You will become like David, who knew his God was bigger than Goliath and did something about it!

This tactics section of your R.I.O.T. Manual is NOT a suggestion list. These aren't just good ideas to read and forget. These are the steps you take to start your Righteous Invasion of Truth. This is an action plan, a smorgasbord of adventure! This is *Indiana Jones, eat your heart out; we're on an adventure for God!*

We'd like you to implement these tactics all the time, but put at least three or four into action each and every week.

Some of the tactics are simple enough that you can do them every day. Some are more complicated and take more time to plan. Carry out at least one MAJOR tactic with your R.I.O.T. Squad each week for four weeks. You want people to hear about God everywhere they turn. Why not? He has been after them for a long time, and it's time we let them know it!

You do not have to finish reading the manual before you start your R.I.O.T. Start planning NOW as you read through the tactics. Go for it. Have a blast and change the world!

1. HIT LIST

A Hit List is the people you target for the Gospel. It's no good to reach "all those people out there somewhere". Go after specific ones. These are the ones you pray God will open their hearts to hear Him. Some people pray a halfhearted prayer and hope that their friends get saved. They might pray, "Dear Lord, please reach Joe." Wow, did you feel the anointing on that? No, and neither did God. God wants us to care enough about people to really pray for them. He wants us to care the same way He does.

Spend some time now putting together your top ten Hit List of people with whom you want to share the Gospel:

1. _____

2. _____

3. _____

4. _____

5. _____

6. _____

7. _____

8. _____

9. _____

10. _____

Now commit to pray for each of them every day. As you pray, ask God what you can say or do to creatively reach them. Listen carefully as you talk with them. You will be amazed at the opportunities God gives you *this week* to talk about Him.

2. EVIDENCE DEMANDS A VERDICT

Theologians (people who study God for a living) have a fancy term for this tactic. They call it *apologetics*. That doesn't mean you're apologizing for believing in God. Apologetics is an explanation of why your beliefs are valid.

Use the Evidence Demands a Verdict tactic when people argue with you about the existence of God. Help them see how small their perspective of God is by asking:

"How many books have you read from cover to cover?"

The answer probably will be "just a few."

Then say, "How many books do you think we have in our library?"

"Probably 10,000."

So you say, "Okay. Now, how many libraries do you think there are in town?"

"Twenty-five libraries."

"How many books do you think are in all of those libraries?"

"Maybe 500,000."

MY FRIEND AND I STAGED A TRIAL— THE PHARISEES V. JESUS. WE WANTED TO USE THE BIBLE AND OTHER BOOKS WRITTEN BY INFORMED CHRISTIANS TO PROVE CHRIST'S CLAIM TO BE THE MESSIAH. I WAS JESUS' LAWYER; MY FRIEND REPRE- SENTED THE PHARISEES. WE HAD A JUDGE, MOTION, OBJEC- TION. IT WAS POW- ERFUL. WE GOT IN EACH OTHER'S FACES AND POUND- ED THE TABLE. IT HELPED OTHERS LEARN HOW TO DEFEND JESUS' CLAIMS USING SCRIPTURE. —LEAH

ONE NOON HOUR AT SCHOOL, WE BROUGHT IN SEVERAL YOUTH PASTORS FROM LOCAL CHURCHES AND HAD A "STUMP THE PASTOR" SESSION. ANY QUESTION, ANY TOPIC!—DEE

"How many libraries do you think there are in the country? And how many books do you think are in all those libraries?"

"Maybe ten million."

"So what you're telling me is that you've read three or four books from cover to cover out of the ten million books that are available. That's how much you know of what there is to be known about scientific facts. That's like saying that you have looked at one piece of sand out of a whole beach full of sand. And because you know what that one piece of sand looks like, you're making a judgment that you know there's no God. If you don't know much about what's already known and written, how can you say with confidence that you know about what's not written? Based on the small amount of information that you have, how can you make a judgment that there cannot possibly be a God who made the whole world?"

The second angle is this: ask them to pray. If they're questioning God's existence, lead them to pray, "Lord, if you're real, show me you're alive." God is big enough and smart enough to know how to get through to them. You know that God will respond because the Bible says "he rewards those who earnestly seek him" (Heb. 11:6). When He does, show your friend how to give his or her heart to Him. God does not cast His pearls before swine. He answers that kind of prayer when He knows a person is ready to receive Him and give his life to Him.

All this evidence of God demands a verdict; it demands that we make a decision. Are we going to give our lives to Jesus or keep our lives to ourselves? We can't *not* make a decision; we decide either for God or against Him.

3. READ THEM THEIR RIGHTS

A police officer reads people their rights to tell them what they are entitled to under the law. When you use the Read

Them Their Rights tactic, you tell people what they are entitled to under God's law of grace.

The gospel is good news, so let's tell people about it. For example:

- **God wants to bless us.** *But seek first his kingdom and his righteousness, and all these things will be given to you as well* (Matt. 6:33).

- **God will give us wisdom when we need it.** *If any of you lacks wisdom, he should ask God, who gives generously to all without finding fault, and it will be given to him* (Jas. 1:5).

- **God will forgive us.** *If we confess our sins, he is faithful and just and will forgive us our sins and purify us from all unrighteousness* (1 John 1:9).

- **God wants to make us new people.** *Therefore, if anyone is in Christ, he is a new creation; the old has gone, the new has come* (2 Cor. 5:17).

The good news is that all people have a right to be free from sin, and to get rid of the garbage the devil has put in their lives. Jesus died so we could be set free, and everyone has a right to know it.

4. Book 'Em

The Book 'Em tactic helps you tactfully share Scripture with others and clearly relate it to their lives. Choose a verse to meditate on during your quiet time in the morning. Then chew on it all day long until it comes alive to you. If you chew on it long enough, the Word of God eventually will explode inside you because it is living and active!

This is when the fun comes in. Start looking for the person God wants you to share that verse with. He has someone waiting that day to hear the Word He put in your heart. Be careful not to dump it on the first person you see. Instead, pray until you find the person God has prepared, then BOOM!

Book 'em! Hit him with the Word in a way that blesses and builds him up. With this tactic, you give a person the right word for the right hour, convincing him that God is real and that He cares for him.

5. WITNESS STAND

The Witness Stand tactic is similar to the weapon of sharing your testimony. A witness stand is where a person is sworn to tell the truth. Use this tactic to share the story of how God changed your life (See "My Testimony," p. 55.)

When you use this tactic, picture yourself on a witness stand before a judge. The person you're testifying before or witnessing to is the jury. Let everything you say about yourself be so believable and powerful that a jury would vote in your favor and say, "Yes, we believe what you say is true." Present yourself so that no one can argue about what God has done in your life. They may respond with philosophy or their opinions but they can't change what you know God has done in your heart.

Be sure to update your testimony regularly so that you're telling not only how you were saved but what God has done recently. During your quiet time, think about what God has done that week so you are always ready to share it (see 1 Peter 3:15).

6. CARMAN CONCERT MANIA

Carman Concert Mania is going absolutely crazy over getting people to the Carman concert in your town. (See R.I.O.T. Tour dates in the back of this manual.) Once you get people to the concert, they will hear the Gospel in a unique way. For those you have shared your faith with for a long time but for some reason haven't said yes, this is a chance to help push them over the edge.

Don't just invite friends and hope they show up at the concert. Make plans to *go with them*. Keep reminding them that the concert is coming up. As the concert date gets closer, your R.I.O.T. Squad should go crazy making sure everyone knows that Carman is coming to town. Use this tactic to invade the Carman concert with a massive bunch of heathens who then are exposed to the gospel and can make a radical commitment to the Lord.

7. PDA (Public Display of Anointing)

WE DID A DRAMA TO "THE CHAMPION" BY CARMAN. WE HAD DEMONS, ANGELS, JESUS, GOD AND SATAN. IT WAS POWERFUL.
—LORI

The PDA tactic can be a blast. The idea is to publicly display the gospel in a way that draws an incredible amount of attention and interest. Once a week plan a major activity for your R.I.O.T. Squad in front of your school before school starts. As students and teachers walk by, they stop and watch because you capture their attention.

Try holding a mock funeral—with a casket

even!—in front of your school. Use music and a whole funeral service. In the middle of it, someone jumps out of the casket and tells the crowd, "I'm alive, like Jesus is alive today."

With your R.I.O.T. Squad, brainstorm other things you can do to act out the gospel. You might build a person-sized Bible that opens up to reveal someone dressed to look like Jesus, who says, "The Word became flesh." Or come dressed like you're going to a toga party and use your clothes to get people's attention while you talk about God. You could hold signs and act like you're picketing. Do whatever will get people's attention. Teens will look forward to the PDA if it is creative and fun. Even though they aren't yet believers, they will appreciate a skit that is attention-getting and thought-provoking.

WE HAD PEOPLE ACT OUT DIFFERENT SINS (LIKE PORNOGRAPHY, PROFANITY, ALCOHOLISM) TO SHOW WHY THE SINS ARE WRONG. THEN WE HAD A JESUS CHARACTER COME AND SHOW THAT SIN SEPARATES US FROM HIM BECAUSE HE IS HOLY. BUT HE ALSO SHOWED THAT HE WOULD BREAK THROUGH THE SIN BARRIER WHEN WE ACCEPT HIM.
—PAOLA

8. RESCUE 911

The Rescue 911 tactic is watching for people who are crying out for help. There are people all around us who are hurting, but we don't always recognize their cries. Some kids feel no one cares about them—not God, not their parents, not *anyone*. Some even think about ending their lives.

You can tell if people are hurting by observing their behavior or listening to what they say. If they always put themselves down, are depressed or never smile, they may need help.

The problem is, we often don't know what to say to them. We try, "Have a nice day," or maybe, "I'll think good thoughts for you," or even, "I'll pray for you." But these folks need more. Be ready at all times to give answers to hurting people. Help them understand that Jesus is the answer to their prayers, the One who can fill their emptiness and put their lives back together.

Rescue 911 may mean you cry with people or pray with them. Some of your own friends may feel their lives are like eggshells that could crack at any moment. Go to them with the compassion of Christ, put your arms around them and pray with them. Let them know that when they give their hearts to Jesus, they will have His arms around them all the time.

FOUR OF US WENT TO AN EMER- GENCY ROOM ALL NIGHT LONG AND MINIS- TERED AND SAW PEO- PLE ACCEPT THE LORD. —JYL

9. DOMESTIC VIOLENCE

Families can experience difficulty between husband and wife or between parents and children. When things grow violent police are called to homes to stop domestic violence.

The Domestic Violence tactic identifies people who are having intense family struggles, then defuses the situation using the gospel. There are young people all around you whose families are falling apart. Their parents are divorced or are going through a divorce. Maybe the parents are together but the kid doesn't feel close to them. Whatever the specifics, they're having a tough time at home.

When you touch on family issues, you will see people's hearts melt. They begin to break down because they realize they don't have all the answers.

Look for clues in the way people talk about their families. Pay attention to how they treat each other at home. When they talk to their parents on the phone, listen to their tone of voice. Pick up on the clues they give and use them to help you lead hurting people to Jesus.

Use Scriptures like these whenever appropriate:

[God is] a father to the fatherless. (Ps. 68:5)

*He will turn the hearts of the fathers to their
children, and the hearts of the children to the
fathers.* (Mal. 4:6)

Because so many people are hurting over family problems,
Domestic Violence could be one of the most effective tactics
in this manual. God made the family and He will put it back
together if we let Him.

10. R.I.O.T. GEAR

The R.I.O.T. Gear tactic simply is wearing clothes that help
start godly conversations. Do the T-shirts and hats you wear
provoke a conversation? Do you ever doodle God stuff on the
bottoms of your shoes for others to read? You can order official R.I.O.T. Gear (see order form in back of this manual) so all
your R.I.O.T. Squad members can dress the same. Or you can
create your own R.I.O.T.-causing clothing.

When you shop for clothes, don't buy stuff because it's

cool or has neat art. Buy clothes that will stop people in their tracks and get them asking questions. Be prepared to give an account for what you're wearing and help lead others to Jesus. There are a number of sources for shirts like this, including Carman Ministries, Living Epistles and Teen Mania. Dedicate part of your closet or drawers solely to R.I.O.T. Gear. As you pray and get ready to wear your R.I.O.T. Gear for the day, get your heart and your life ready to be a witnessing machine.

11. INTERROGATION

The Interrogation tactic helps you discover valuable things about a person by asking him questions. Find out all you can about him before you try to get into his heart. *Become a learner.* Learn who he is, where he is from, what he's like, what's important to him, how he spends his time. How's his relationship with his mom or dad? What about brothers and sisters? What are his ambitions, goals and dreams? What is he afraid of? Of course, don't ask all of these questions at once. Just begin to probe and discover as much as you can about him.

People often act as if they have their life together without God. But the truth is that nobody is together without God. Ask questions to find where they are not together. Be tactful as you use the Interrogation tactic. Show a genuine interest in people, so they'll know you care about them and want to bring them to Jesus.

12. CROSS EXAMINATION

Although similar to Interrogation, the Cross Examination tactic asks questions that lead people to the cross. Hence the term, *Cross* Examination. Use the following questions to help a friend think seriously about the Lord:

1. What do you think about God? Who is He? What is He like?

2. How do you think someone can get close to God?

3. What do you think a real Christian is? What's your definition of a real Christian?

4. Do you mind if I tell you the Bible's definition of a real Christian?

If you ask those questions and she says, "No, I don't mind," share the gospel very simply. Begin by telling her what the Bible says: "All have sinned and fallen short of the glory of God" (Rom. 3:23). Then tell her God wants to give her a new heart and life and to forgive her sin and make her a new person. You can say things like,

> *Becoming a Christian doesn't happen because you are born into a Christian*

nation or your parents are Christians. You make a decision to give your life to the Lord, and you're never the same again.

Give a brief (two-to-three minute) description of what it means to give your life to the Lord. Talk especially about the miracle that happens, how God totally changes you on the inside. Then ask this question:

5. Is there anything keeping you from giving your life to Jesus?

If she says no, then the sixth question you ask is:

6. Would you like to pray right now and give your heart to the Lord?

Your questions lead her to the cross so she can give her life to the Lord. Then, get her into church and youth group so that others can help her grow spiritually.

13. Captive Audience

I RAN FOR STUDENT BODY PRESIDENT ON COLOSSIANS 3:17. IT WAS ON MY POSTERS AND I TALKED ABOUT MY RELATIONSHIP WITH JESUS CHRIST IN MY SPEECH. GOD NOT ONLY REACHED OTHERS THROUGH THIS, BUT SHOWED ME HIS FAITHFULNESS. I WON!
— CHARLIEANN

Implement the Captive Audience tactic whenever you give a speech or presentation or write a paper for class. Don't let a chance like that go by without talking about the Lord. It takes courage and guts and needs to be done creatively. You don't have to share a sermon, just weave God into whatever your topic is. You have a captive audience; they can't go anywhere. They have to listen to you, so give them something worth listening to and remembering.

This is how I (Ron) handled it one time. I had to give a speech in class on the military draft. For the first minute or so, I discussed the draft and what it was. Then I talked about how God doesn't draft people into heaven. He has an army, but it is made up of volunteers. He doesn't force you to go to heaven. You've got to join; He'll never draft you. It's up to you.

Don't be afraid to write about Jesus in your class papers. You can witness to your teacher, and practice articulating what you believe.

14. MALL BLITZ

With the Mall Blitz tactic, your R.I.O.T. Squad infiltrates a shopping mall. Be careful with this one—some security guards may see this as harassing the customers. In a Mall Blitz, you arm yourself with tracts, then march through the mall handing them out and going crazy letting people know that Jesus loves them.

This has been tried with more than a thousand kids at a time in one mall. Although you probably won't have that many people, go in with the idea of completely canvassing

MY FRIEND'S YOUTH GROUP GOT HOLD OF A HEARSE SOMEHOW AND DROVE IT TO A MALL. WHEN THEY GOT THERE, SOME-ONE DRESSED AS THE GRIM REAPER JUMPED OUT OF THE HEARSE. THIS GOT EVERY-ONE'S ATTEN-TION. THEN THEY DID A DRAMA AND HAD A CHANCE FOR PEOPLE TO ACCEPT THE LORD. —AARON the mall. Leave tracts with every person and in every place you can. For example, go into bookstores and place them inside books, so when people buy a book they also get a tract. Put tracts in the hands of mannequins and in pockets of pants. It's exciting to think you can massively impact a number of people with a message from the Lord, helping them become God-conscious and leading them closer to making a decision for Jesus.

15. Radio Contact

This tactic already has been proven effective by teens. First, R.I.O.T. Squad members rent some pagers. Then print on a business card something like this:

> **Need to talk? Need prayer?**
> **Need somebody to help?**
> **Give me a call day or night.**
> **I'm here for you.**
> **(your name)**
> **(pager #)**

Pass the cards out everywhere you go. You will be amazed to see the response from those who won't talk to you about the Lord in public. When they get alone and quiet, they want to talk to you. They'll call you with some deep questions, serious concerns—things you can help them with. It's exciting to be on a mission from God, waiting to answer a page at any moment from someone in crisis. Radio Contact is a way to show people you mean business about caring for them.

16. STING OPERATION

In a Sting Operation your R.I.O.T. Squad conspires to minister to a specific person. You watch where that person hangs out and what he is into. You pray together for that person and get creative about how you will get the gospel to him.

Think about how to approach him with the Word in different places at different times of the day. You put a tract in his locker; your friend puts one on his car. You invite him to a Christian event, and then your R.I.O.T. Squad friends all invite him to the same event at different times during the day. In other words, gang up on him. Let a series of polite initiatives let him know that you are praying for him and that God loves him. The person may not even realize that you are working together. You all work on his heart until you know it is softened and he's ready to receive the Lord. This could take longer than other tactics, but in the end you will win by demonstrating that you love and respect him.

17. RACE R.I.O.T.

Our Race R.I.O.T. is not the same as what happened in Los Angeles. This is simply a Righteous Invasion of Truth among all races. God wants us to love each other and treat each other respectfully. The truth is we are all born in sin and are equally lost without Jesus. Jesus forgives us and makes us all new creations once we give our lives to Him.

The question is not "Are you black, brown or white?" The question is "Are you *red*?" Are you covered in Jesus's blood? Where will you spend eternity? That is the question!

The best way to incite a Race R.I.O.T. is by demonstrating a different kind of relationship between the races. Here's how to do that: Find someone of a different race and do everything you can to be a friend to that person. Really get to know her. Share your heart with her. Learn to appreciate, not make fun of, your differences.

The devil has distracted us from the big picture of winning the whole world and got us fighting each other instead of fighting the fight of faith. Find some friends of another race and either win them to Jesus or, if they're already saved, ask them to join your R.I.O.T. Squad. You'll be surprised how your attitudes toward other races will change, and how all of you together will change the world!

18. BEHIND ENEMY LINES

This tactic is sure to get your adventurous side charged up! It will take you right where the lost are. The Bible says our enemy is the devil; Behind Enemy Lines is a tactic to infiltrate people who follow him.

In most towns you'll find Mormon or Jehovah's Witnesses churches. There are other cults represented in almost every city in America. Find tracts that address the cult's perspective of life from a Biblical viewpoint, then go Behind Enemy

Lines—into their church buildings. When the building is open, go in and pray and bind the devil. Then, discreetly insert tracts into books in their pews. When they have their next service, those who see the tracts will get a surprise that could give them a new life!

19. POINT MAN

A point man is "one who is in the forefront" or "a soldier who goes ahead of a patrol."[13] The Point Man tactic goes after the person others look to for leadership at school or work. You know, the few who naturally influence others around them. These people are either natural leaders or have become popular because of their talents and abilities.

The strategy is this: Your R.I.O.T. Squad targets a point man others look up to. Once you have successfully reached him, he can then influence a lot of others with the gospel. This person may be harder to reach because of all the sup-

---

13 *Webster's Tenth New Collegiate Dictionary,* Merriam-Webster, 1993.

posed "success" he has on the outside. The fact is, though, every person without Jesus is empty on the inside. If you get to know enough about your point man you probably will find he is empty, too. When you dis- cover that, then you will have a door into his heart.

This point man is no more important than all the people he influences. You are not going after the point man because God loves him more, but because God loves all the people he can help influence. Check your motives: be sure you target your point man because you have a genuine love for him from the Lord, not because you want to be the one known for reaching the big cheese. As you keep your motives right, you could reach a lot of people by reaching one point man!

20. STREET DRAMA

The purpose of street drama is to invite people into your world. They stop and watch you because they want to see what you're about. During those moments when you have their attention, you can make your time count.

Street drama doesn't have to be complicated. It could be as simple as one of your R.I.O.T. Squad members falling on the ground pretending to be choking. You fall down beside her and ask, "Does anyone know CPR?" Another R.I.O.T. Squad member runs up while everyone is gathering around. When you have everyone's attention say,

THERE WERE KIDS IN OUR YOUTH GROUP WHO DIDN'T KNOW HOW TO GET SAVED. SO, WE STAGED A TALK SHOW (LIKE "OPRAH"). I ACTED AS A DRUG ADDICT ON THE SHOW, AND ANOTHER PERSON PLANTED IN THE AUDIENCE LED ME TO JESUS.
—JOSH

This is what most of the world is doing. They're choking, but they don't even know it. They're

dying on the inside and feel totally empty. They need someone to give them CPR. And that is exactly what Jesus did. He came to give us a new heart and new life. We want you to know that if you feel like you're choking today, God loves you and so do we, and we want to tell you more about Him.

A skit like that can draw people to the Lord and get them thinking about eternal issues. Make one up yourself, or use prepared skits. Don't be afraid to try a complicated, well-choreographed drama with costumes and makeup. Impact Productions and Teen Mania Ministries (see Resources p.148) can give you information if your R.I.O.T. Squad is interested in performing a drama like that. You can find other less ambitious skits for impromptu situations in your local Christian bookstore. Be creative about where and when you do Street Drama.

21. VIDEO SURVEILLANCE

Here is another unique tactic for getting into people's hearts. Take your R.I.O.T. Squad out with a video camera and do interviews at the mall, at school, at a ball game or at a local hangout. Walk up to a group of people and tell them you're making a video program. You aren't lying—just don't say it's going to be on T.V. Ask them if you can videotape them. Most people will agree.

WE WENT TO A TEEN HANGOUT WITH A COOLER FULL OF COLD SODAS AND CANDY BARS AND A VIDEO CAMERA EQUIPPED WITH A MICRO-PHONE. WE PASSED OUT THE GOODIES WHILE THE M.C. ASKED THE CROWD QUES-TIONS LIKE, "WHO'S A HERO TO YOU?" OR "WHAT'S LOVE?" THEN WE CONCLUDED BY TELLING THEM ABOUT JESUS. (WE HAD A PRAYER WARRIOR PRAYING WHILE THE STREET GROUP WAS OUT MINISTERING.) —BRADLEY

Have one person hold the video camera and the other person interview. Ask them the questions we discussed in Cross Examination, p. 85.

Then take two to three minutes and share the gospel with them. Putting it in a nutshell, tell them how God wants to forgive them and change them from the inside out. While you are still taping, ask them if they think that would be a good thing for a person to do. Watch their responses. If they say *yes*, ask them if they want to do it right now. You can pray right there and God absolutely will change their hearts and lives. You'll be amazed at how many people will pray with you with the videotape rolling and miracles happening before your eyes. When you are done, invite them to come to your youth group.

Take the videotape back to your youth group and show them what God is doing. It is a unique way to get the gospel out and have a great recording for later. It is amazing how the video camera can get people to answer questions and say things they may never have said if you approached them in conversation. It gives you an excuse to talk to people you don't know, because you are "making a video program."

22. APB (ALL POINTS BULLETIN)

Police use an APB to get out an announcement to anyone with a police radio. You can use the APB tactic to get out the message of the gospel in a massive way to your whole school. Most schools have written or spoken announcements on a regular basis. An APB enables you to spread the news that your R.I.O.T. Squad is alive and that God is doing something in your hearts. If it is against the rules at your school to mention *Jesus* or *God*, simply release an APB about all of the R.I.O.T. Squad meetings and activities.

There are other ways you can use an APB to let people know that God is alive and loves them. Tag your R.I.O.T. announcements with something like this:

- When you feel no one cares, God does.

- When you come to the end of your rope, there is Someone to catch you.

- When exams get tough, it's good to know Someone's there to help.

Start your APB with "Another Announcement from your R.I.O.T. Squad...," so they know it's coming from you and they know the meaning of the phrases. The point is to continually have them hear or see something about the Lord so they get the idea God loves them and is after them.

23. Public Propaganda

Use this tactic to get a lot of attention in a short amount of time. Public Propaganda is getting a message to the public in a big way. Use this tactic at sports events or any major public gathering. Have your R.I.O.T. Squad make a huge banner with a simple line that makes people think. For example:

Do you know where you would go if you died tonight?

or

It is the year 2090. Do you know where your soul is?

Put the banner where it will be seen (by the goal post?). Go through the crowd and ask people what they think of the banner. It will start conversations.

This is your opportunity to help people become God conscious. If they are going to remember that God is near, they need to see and hear that message everywhere they go. It will make them think about serious issues and will pave the way for important discussions.

24. ROLLER BLADE BLITZ

The Roller Blade Blitz tactic is for you sporting types who like to live on the edge. This tactic gives you a chance to get into a person's world and become a Jew to a Jew, a Greek to a Greek, or as Paul would have said had he lived today, a roller blader to a roller blader (see 1 Cor. 9:20).

The tactic works like it sounds: Put on your roller blades and your protective gear, and stuff your pockets full of tracts (your concealed weapons). You and your R.I.O.T. Squad go hang out for a couple of hours where the skaters are. As you cruise through the area you're like an invading mob with good news. As you skate by, hand a tract to every person you see—people on benches, people walking down the street, people roller blading with you. It is a free-for-all, a blitz, so every person in the area is invaded with the gospel as you go blazing through on your blades.

25. S.W.A.T. Team

The S.W.A.T. Team tactic works much like a special police force called in to attack a situation. *S.W.A.T.* stands for *S*pecial *W*eapons *A*nd *T*actics Team or a *S*pecial *W*eapons *A*ttack *T*eam. Your R.I.O.T. Squad can become a S.W.A.T. Team and take over a spiritual situation.

Here is how this tactic works: Find out what events are happening in your area and choose one for your R.I.O.T. Squad to attend. Prepare for the event by assigning every person an area to cover. You'll need everyone if you are to have full coverage of the event. When you arrive at the event, infiltrate the place. Everybody takes his or her position so that no one gets away without seeing or hearing the gospel.

Choose events your R.I.O.T. Squad can cover, so that not one person will leave without hearing about the Lord. The S.W.A.T. Team tactic is adventurous and exciting, so have a blast as you target places in your world with the gospel.

26. HIGH-SPEED CHASE

Police embark on a high-speed chase when somebody needs to be caught immediately. Perhaps a person is driving drunk or has just committed a crime. In any case, they need to be apprehended now.

This is exactly what happens when you use the High-speed Chase tactic with your R.I.O.T. Squad. You see somebody at school or work who is in big trouble. She is not her normal self. You can tell by the way she talks and acts that she's hurting. Maybe her grades are messed up. Maybe she hasn't been coming to class or youth group like she used to. You've heard she's been doing drugs and that they are now messing up her life. There is a big-time reason to go after her, so implement the High-speed Chase.

Start by bombarding her with prayer from your R.I.O.T. Squad. You could even start a 24-hour prayer chain with your church so someone is constantly praying for her. Focus on chasing that person down and giving her the gospel. Begin to hang out with her and go places with her. Sit next to her in class and start conversations. Ask all the other R.I.O.T. Squad members to do the same. Relentlessly pursue this person until you know you've got a good dose of the gospel in her. Don't give up until she has responded positively to it. Don't gun her down; open up your heart and care about what she's going through.

As you walk through your school or your workplace, the Holy Spirit may put somebody on your heart whom you can't forget. Pray for that person with your R.I.O.T. Squad. Then go after her. Give everything you've got to reach her for the Lord. Don't stop until she's heard that Jesus can help her out of the time of trouble. This is a high-speed chase of a holy kind. And there are people around you right now who desperately need it.

27. R.I.O.T. Movie

The R.I.O.T. Movie tactic could influence your whole school. This is how it works: Find an auditorium at school you can use, perhaps after school or during lunch. Then rent a movie with a strong evangelical message. There are a number of movies out that help kids know more about the Lord. Some suggestions are Mars Hill Productions' *Without Reservation,* any Billy Graham movie, *China Cry,* and others. Check with Gospel Films (see Resources, p. 144) for rental information. Be sure you watch the film beforehand to make sure it is just the right one.

When you have the right movie, set up a time to show it at school. Put up posters and fliers, make an announcement and invite everyone to come. Serve free popcorn and try to get somebody to donate soft drinks. A good time would be during lunch; just make sure the lunch period is long enough to show the movie you have. You don't want people walking out during the good part, and you don't want to encourage anyone to skip classes.

Give enough advance notice so that people can plan ahead for the showing. Make sure you have a large screen, not a T.V. monitor. Show the film on a video projector so people get a real movie vibe. Be ready for someone to bring in the net or give a short altar call right after the movie is over.

28. POST-MOVIE BLITZ

A number of recent movies have had spiritual overtones. Some speculate on heaven; some feature a Christian in a leading role or refer openly to God. A movie like *Ghost* can cause viewers to think about what happens after death. *Forrest Gump* can make you think about what your life really counts for and how ordinary people can do great things.

These movies that affect people emotionally can set the stage for your Squad to launch a witnessing blitz. Find a tract that deals with the movie, or a general evangelistic tract, and hang out outside the movie theater. Share the tracts in a tactful way with the audience as they leave. This is a prime opportunity to talk about God because they are already thinking about eternal things. Say things like,

> *Did seeing that movie make you think about where you're going to go when you die?*
>
> *How do you think people get to heaven?*

After *Forrest Gump*, you could say,

> *Isn't it amazing how so many of us feel like*

Forrest Gump, like we aren't special? But God thinks we're special. Jesus came in the same way. People didn't think He was important or special, but He ended up changing the world and He can change your heart.

If you want to live on the edge, sit on the front row of the theater during the movie. As soon as the movie is over, stand up and say, "Excuse me. Before you leave, we have a few announcements to make." Take two or three minutes to share the gospel before people leave. Some people might walk out, but you may be able to make the audience think both about the point of the movie and about the gospel. You might even give an alter call. Say, "If you'd like to receive the Lord, raise your hand and I'll pray with you." Use what Hollywood puts in people's minds to make them think about eternity.

29. LOCKER INVASION

The Locker Invasion tactic simply means your R.I.O.T. Squad puts tracts in every locker in your school. Think about doing it after hours so you don't irritate people. It's an opportunity to impact every kid in your school in a single day.

You might decide to use this tactic regularly—once a week or month. But be creative and use a different tract each time. When there is a Carman concert or a youth event coming up, use the tickets as tracts. On one side print the gospel, on the other side advertise the event, then shove them through those slots. Why do you think they put slots on lockers—for ventilation only? No way! They're there to help you get the gospel into people's lives.

30. BATHROOM REVIVAL

Face it, when people are in the bathroom, they think about something. By implementing the Bathroom Revival tactic, you can encourage them to think about how much God loves them and where they will spend eternity.

Make a sign that says something simple yet thought-provoking, like the banners in Public Propaganda. Tape it to the inside of a stall or somewhere else where people will see it. Even if they wouldn't normally read a tract, they'll read this one while they're sitting there.

Another Bathroom Revival tactic is putting tracts in the toilet paper dispenser. If you have the roll-up kind, unroll it and put the tracts in one at a time as you roll it back up. As the paper is unrolled, the tracts will fall out one at a time.

Help people understand that no matter where they are or what they're doing God sees them and wants their hearts.

31. REAL FOOD

Use the Real Food tactic to get the gospel into people's hearts during lunch time in your cafeteria. Standing in line for lunch at school usually is a brain-dead activity. But you can infiltrate the cafeteria by putting a tract on every tray before people pick them up.

As they're holding their tray in line, they will begin to read the tract and find out more about the Lord. When they reach for a napkin, they'll pick up a tract because you've infiltrated the napkin holders with tracts. After a while people will get the message that there is an invasion going on in their school—a Righteous Invasion of Truth.

32. STAKEOUT

With the Stakeout tactic, you will watch closely the person you want to witness to, much as police watch a suspected criminal. What do you watch for? You look for clues that will tell you what your "suspect" believes or thinks is important. For example, if he spends a lot of time messing with his hair or clothes that tells you something about him. It could mean he is insecure and doesn't have a high opinion of himself. Maybe you notice that he looks sad all the time or that he cuts himself down frequently. As a result, you could share the gospel by telling him that God sees him as incredibly valuable.

Maybe you notice that one of the people you're praying for dresses like a certain music group. If you want to relate to her, read up on the lyrics of that kind of music. Find a song that has some spiritual overtones and find out what the Bible has to say about that subject. When you get a chance, ask her, "So, what do you think *[her favorite band]* means when they say _____?" Listen to her ideas, then gently tell her what the Bible says.

By closely observing people you can pick up clues that can help you present the gospel to them in a unique way. Some have blasted others with the gospel and shoved the Bible down their throats before they took the time to know them. But a Stakeout is loving people enough to learn how they see life before you tell them about the Lord.

33. JAIL MINISTRY

The Jail Ministry tactic can take your R.I.O.T. Squad into a county jail for adults or a detention center for teens to share the gospel. While there, use drama, music and tracts to reach a captive audience.

Plan a Jail Ministry by first talking to your youth pastor. If you can't find anyone at your church to help, try contacting the facility directly. Ask the chaplain if your Squad can come out on a Saturday afternoon. Most chaplains in juvenile institutions are happy to have people visit who are good role models for kids. When you go, be ready to minister. The chaplain can help you choose the R.I.O.T. tactics most appropriate for his or her institution.

A GIRL IN MY YOUTH GROUP WROTE A MODERN-DAY VERSION OF THE CHRISTMAS STORY. WE CHOREOGRAPHED DANCE AND MUSIC AND SIGN LANGUAGE ALONG WITH DRAMA. WE TOOK IT TO A BOYS' CORRECTIONAL FACILITY AT CHRISTMAS. LOTS OF KIDS GOT SAVED AND WERE DISCIPLED OVER TIME BY RETURNING MINISTRY GROUPS. —MELISSA

One More Thing . . .

When you share the gospel, choose one tactic and stick with it. Using several tactics at once could confuse the issue. If you choose to use the Cross Examination tactic, stick with the plan. Don't get so stirred up in the middle of asking questions that you share your testimony. You'll most likely confuse the person.

Part 4

ZONES

1. PERSONAL LIFE

The first place we should see a Righteous Invasion of Truth is in our own lives. We need constantly to be invaded with the power of God through the Word. We ought to be living examples of God's truth—transparent, holy examples for the world to emulate. In other words, if we want to start a R.I.O.T., we have to let a R.I.O.T. start in us.

What does that mean? It means that every day we make sure Jesus is Lord of every part of our lives. Is Jesus your Boss, your Chief, your Commander, the One you answer to? This is no flighty little decision made one day at the altar when our emotions are high. We live for Him every day with all our hearts. We have the Word of God living big inside us so that we become reflections of what the Bible says.

Here are some tactics you can use to help you stay full of God's truth and fire:

- **Have a quiet time every day.** That may mean getting up earlier than usual. Before you get ready for school or work, read the Word, pray and seek God. Don't just read a few stories from the Bible and call it done; *really* read it and ask God what He is saying to you today. For example, how do you apply this to your life? What can you take with you today that you can chew on all day? Memorize some Scriptures each morning and pray about the things you will encounter that day. Pray about the R.I.O.T. tactics you want to implement. Your quiet time is important—it fills you up and gives you fuel for the rest of the day.

- **Listen to teaching tapes.** Don't rely only on your church to get fed. Listen to tapes of different speakers who will teach you about the Lord. Select tapes on subjects you are weak in so you'll get stronger in that area. Radically, passionately, go after the truth, cramming it in your heart and brain.

- **Take sermon notes.** Every time you hear a sermon, write things down. Keep what you write in a notebook so you can refer to it later. Go back through your notes and pray about what you've written. Do a study in the Scripture on the topic. Taking notes helps build up your life with God. If you write things down, you do more than just listen. The thoughts go through your head and out your hand. You listen more carefully and process more.

2. HOME

What does it mean to have a Righteous Invasion of Truth at home? It means that everything that happens in your home is an example of righteousness. Make sure the T.V. programs and videos you watch are holy. Make sure all your habits at home are holy.

We need a Righteous Invasion of Truth in our relationships with our parents and our brothers and sisters. Treat them in a holy and honorable way before God. Be submissive and forgiving when someone does you wrong.

Don't merely tolerate one another. God is the source of your power. He has forgiven you and made you brand new. So let His love invade your relationships with your family.

3. SCHOOL

Where do we need a Righteous Invasion of Truth more than in our schools? Whether you go to a junior or senior high school, God longs to be there. He loves your classmates, teachers and administrators, and your job is to let them know it. Public school has long been the devil's playground and a place for him to call the shots about what is cool and popular. And a lot of kid's lives have been messed up. It is time for us, the army of the living God, to make ourselves known. Here are a few tactics you can implement in your school:

- **Start a Bible Club at your school, if you don't already have one.** The Supreme Court says it is lawful for you to have one. Call it a R.I.O.T. Squad if you want, so people realize this isn't just another Bible

Club where they sit and get blessed. Let them know your club is here to cause a R.I.O.T.

- **Have a R.I.O.T. party after school.** Once a month or so, show a video like *Time 2* or some other fun, full-length music video. Serve refreshments and use the time to minister.

Also, many of the tactics we described in Part 3 directly apply to your school. As a teenager, most of your time will be spent in school. So from sun up to sun down, let people know that there is a group of radical young warriors ready to cause a R.I.O.T. It is time for people to realize that God is alive and on the scene. He lives in the hearts of thousands of fired-up, wild teenagers who refuse to compromise their walk with God.

4. FRIENDS

The Friends zone is an especially important place to have a R.I.O.T. It is easy to talk about changing the world and doing something for God when you're together with a bunch of other Christians. But when you're with friends who don't know the Lord, it's a whole different thing. No matter what someone thinks, no matter how "good" a friend he is, be sure you are more committed to Jesus. If you really care about your friend and love him for who he is, then tell him the truth.

We have given you so many tactics to use, it will be easy for you to creatively get the truth across to your friends. Regularly use them in your friendships so that all of your friends know you are a Christian and that you are forcefully advancing the kingdom of God. Your friends who don't know the Lord need to hear the gospel from you. The friends who do know the Lord need to participate in the R.I.O.T., helping stir up others to know God.

5. WORKPLACE

A R.I.O.T. should spread to everything you are part of—even your work. Many of the tactics we have talked about can be implemented at work. But show discretion when implementing a R.I.O.T. tactic at work; you could lose your job if you do too much. This is where you need to hear the Holy Spirit. If you lose your job you will not have the opportunity to minister to that group of people anymore. However, if you compromise you may have a tough time living with yourself knowing those people will go to hell while you did nothing to prevent it. Be sensitive to God. Bring in a R.I.O.T., but do it respectfully without offending others.

You might share your faith with your supervisor. Or you may have to refuse to do something your boss asks you to do because it goes against Scripture. It may cost you your job, but that's better than their losing salvation for eternity. Blaze a trail by starting a Bible study at work. Come a few minutes early and study the Bible with those who are interested in hearing more about the Lord. God has put you in your job for a reason. Take advantage of the opportunity. Make it count for eternity and invade your work with a R.I.O.T.

6. CHURCH

Is your church youth group fired up with a passion to serve God? If not, you need a Righteous Invasion of Truth. If your church is not fired up, most likely it is not your pastor's fault. Your pastor probably has been looking a long time for someone who will live the principles he's talked about all these years. Why don't you help your pastor stir up a Righteous Invasion of Truth?

Meet with your pastor and tell him that you want to implement some of these tactics as a youth group. Maybe a smaller group of fired-up members of your youth group can start the R.I.O.T. Squad, and then go crazy implementing tactics all over the region. God is tired of youth groups full of a bunch of slow-motion, candy-coated Christians who come to church because they are forced to. Somebody who has caught the fire of God needs to stand up and say, "Just a minute! We're going to do this the way God designed it. We're going to change the world!" Don't be intimidated by what others might think about you. Go for it.

7. COMMUNITY

Let the community at large know that Jesus is alive in the hearts of your R.I.O.T. Squad. Here are some practical ways to target your community:

- **Perform community service projects.** Pick up litter on the sides of the road, clean up a park or help with an elderly home project. Make sure you express the gospel to the people you serve. Let people see that you care about your community because Jesus is alive inside of you.

- **Petition your local cable company.** Get signatures of people who want to see MTV taken off the air. Ask area church members to sign petitions saying they will cancel their cable unless they take MTV out of your region. There are documented cases where this has worked. Try this radical R.I.O.T. tactic, and keep your community from being brainwashed with MTV.

8. GOVERNMENT

You may be young, but you can start a Righteous Invasion of Truth in our government. First of all, the Bible tells us to pray for all those in authority (see 1 Tim. 2:1-2). You can pray for our president, your senators and congressional representatives, and all the people who rule over you. Be in the know about how government affects your right to share your faith. Here are two things you can do to influence the government to change:

- **Sign a petition.** Last year on *The Standard* tour, Carman gathered one million names on a petition that said, "We want prayer back in school." You could circulate a petition regarding some other godly issue, then send it to your elected officials.

- **Vote.** As you prepare to turn eighteen, start tracking now what's going on in politics. Study who's righteous, who's unrighteous, who loves the Lord and lives like it, and who doesn't. By the time you're ready to vote, you won't vote for some airhead who mumbles something about being born-again. You'll know to vote for candidates who will live out in office what is in their hearts.

9. WORLD

This R.I.O.T. Zone probably is overlooked by teens more than any other. But God calls us as a young, committed, fiery army to invade the whole world with His truth. It is time to quit hogging the good news to ourselves here in America, in our church or our family. It is time to take it to the world.

IT'S TRUE, NOW'S THE TIME TO WIN NATIONS
FOR THE LORD

IT'S TRUE, NOW'S THE HOUR, THE SAINTS
MUST GO TO WAR

AND, WE'LL PREACH IT, WE'LL SING IT, WE'LL
SHOUT IT, WE'LL CRY IT

'CAUSE DESPERATE TIMES NEED DESPERATE
ACTION AND THAT MEANS WE NEED A
R.I.O.T. [14]

Let's quit talking about the world, and get out and reach
it. Let's quit reading books and singing about reaching the
world, and do it. It starts with you and me. A R.I.O.T. changes
our perspective of what our lives are about. We are living in

---

14 Lyrics from "R.I.O.T." by Carman. © 1995 Some-O-Dat Music (admin. by Word, Inc.) (BMI)/Bases Loaded Music/Sierra Sky Songs (Bases Loaded Music and Sierra Sky Songs admin. by EMI Christian Music Publishing) (ASCAP) All rights reserved. Used by permission.

this world to make a difference in it. In many parts of the world there are people who have never heard of Jesus. Even with all the Christian T.V., radio, conferences and concerts, still there are 1.3 billion people who have never had a chance to hear the gospel. If we claim to be people who are committed to the Lord to change the world, then it is time for us to do something about it. There are several tactics you can use to reach your world:

- **Pray.** Pray for the nations of the world, and pray for people who have never had a chance to hear the gospel. Ask God to heal their broken lives. Read books like *Operation World* by Patrick Johnstone (Zondervan) that can teach you more about different countries. Pray for those countries and the people in them who have never been reached.

- **Send someone.** Many young people want to serve in another country, but can't because they don't have the money. When you raise funds to send a friend on a mission trip, you are helping start a R.I.O.T. in a nation without God's truth. Every R.I.O.T. Squad should plan to send at least one member on a mission trip each summer. Everyone else in the Squad can rally around that one and help raise the money. Work as passionately as if you were going yourself. Put feet to your words. Let's take the R.I.O.T. to the world!

- **Go.** "Me? Go on a mission trip?" Why not? You may never have thought about going. Or maybe you've wondered how you would get the money, or if your parents would let you go. There are a lot of reasons why you *shouldn't* go. But there are 1.3 billion reasons why we *must* go: that many people are on their way to hell without a chance of hearing the truth unless somebody tells them.

Why not do something different this summer? Go on a mission trip instead of to camp or just hanging out. Or work half the summer, then go on a mission trip the last half.

Everybody should experience a short mission trip at least once. When you go and share your faith with people and see their lives changed, you realize God can use you to affect others for eternity.

> WELL ALL RIGHT, OKAY, I GUESS IT'S UP, UP AND
>   AWAY!
>
> I'M TAKIN' A STEP, A TAKIN' A STEP OF FAITH
>
> WALKIN' OUT ON THE PROMISES GOD MADE
>
> TAKIN' A GIANT LEAP IN THE AIR
>
> STEPPIN' OUT ON NOTHIN' AND FINDIN' SOMETHIN'
>   THERE
>
> TELLIN' THE DOUBT TO WAIT, WAIT, WAIT, WAIT
>
> I'M TAKIN' A STEP OF FAITH [15]

If your church takes mission trips, get involved. If you don't know where to go, come on a Teen Mania summer mission trip (see p. 148 in the back of this manual). You could be on your way to starting a R.I.O.T. in a nation somewhere around the world. You could be one of the young people who helps start a church in a little village that has never heard the gospel before.

For God so loved the world . . . He didn't send a fax; He didn't shower down tracts out of heaven; He didn't put a note in a bottle and throw it in the ocean. He sent a person: His own Son Jesus Christ. Only a person could express the love of the Father to the people of the earth. Today, God still so loves the world that He sends people like you and me to go and make a difference. When you wrap your arms around a lost and broken world, you wrap the arms of Jesus around the world.

PART 5

WEAPONS AND TACTICS CHECKLIST

Okay, here it is: the finale, where the whole manual comes together. This is where you plan the weapons and the tactics you will use for each of the different R.I.O.T. Zones. It is time to get involved. Commit to do something—start a Righteous Invasion of Truth.

The minimum goal for each R.I.O.T. Squad is to implement three weapons and three tactics for each R.I.O.T. Zone. That's twenty-seven weapons and twenty-seven tactics put into action. Just imagine what you can do to destroy the devil's plans with that many tactics!

Here's how to go about it: Implement one tactic per week, per zone, for three weeks. Do more if you can. As you plan and implement tactics, write them on the Weapons and Tactics Checklist so that you can watch what you have done and see the fruit of your ministry. There are places to indicate total number of people saved and ministered to. There's also a place to write in the tactics you used in each of the different zones. God bless you and give you a great time as you reach the people around you with a R.I.O.T. in every one of these nine zones.

WEAPONS AND

1. _____ 2. _____
3. _____ 4. _____
5. _____ 6. _____

DATE R.I.O.T. SQUAD WAS FORMED _____

ZONE	Week 1 Date ____		Week 2 Date ____	
	WEAPON	TACTIC	WEAPON	TACTIC
Personal Life				
Home				
School				
Friends				
Work				
Church				
Community				
Government				
World				

Total people witnessed to: _____

Total people saved: _____

Total number of weapons used: _____

Total number of tactics used: _____

TACTICS CHECKLIST

7. _____   8. _____

9. _____   10. _____

11. _____   12. _____

Week 3 Date ____		Week 4 Date ____	
WEAPON	**TACTIC**	**WEAPON**	**TACTIC**

Youth Pastor's Signature _____

Parent's Signature _____

R.I.O.T. Squad Member's Signature _____

R.I.O.T. SQUAD CONTEST

Stir up as big a R.I.O.T. as you can before Carman's R.I.O.T. Tour hits your region. The R.I.O.T. should be raging out of control by the time Carman rolls into town. At the concert, bring all the people you have affected with your R.I.O.T. Bring them to the concert whether or not they have prayed to received Christ. It will be a HUGE coming together of all the R.I.O.T. Squads in the region. Watch out! It's going to blow your face off!

At each R.I.O.T. Concert, Carman will give an award to the R.I.O.T. Squad in that region that has implemented the most weapons and tactics. Just think, it could be your R.I.O.T. Squad Carman calls forward in front of thousands of people to claim the prize!

How do you enter? Simply send a copy of

your Weapons and Tactics Checklist and a list of the names of all your R.I.O.T. Squad members (see p. 145). Have it signed by your youth pastor and include several stories of lives that have been changed by your R.I.O.T. Squad. Your entry must be received no later than ten days before the Carman concert you attend. You could win an incredible award; but more importantly, you will be winning people to Jesus!

RESOURCES

FILMS

Mars Hill Productions
12705 South Kirkwood, Suite 218
Stafford, TX 77477
(800) 580-6579

Gospel Films
(800) 253-0413

STREET DRAMA

Impact Productions
807 S. Xanthus Place
Tulsa, OK 74104
(918) 582-4464

Teen Mania Ministries
P.O. Box 700721
Tulsa, OK 74170-0721
(918) 496-1891

SPRING TOUR DATES

2/12	ODESSA, TX	3/26	TERRE HAUTE, IN
2/13	LUBBOCK, TX	3/28	EVANSVILLE, IN
2/22	LAKE CHARLES, LA	3/29	MEMPHIS, TN
2/23	SHREVEPORT, LA	3/30	KNOXVILLE, TN
2/26	BILOXI, MS	4/9	LITTLE ROCK, AR
2/27	PENSACOLA, FL	4/11	SPRINGFIELD, MO
2/29	JACKSONVILLE, FL	4/12	COLUMBIA, MO
3/1	JACKSONVILLE, FL	4/13	CINCINNATI, OH
3/2	TALLAHASSEE, FL	4/16	FORT WAYNE, IN
3/4	ALBANY, GA	4/18	E. LANSING, MI
3/5	SAVANNAH, GA	4/19	CLEVELAND, OH
3/7	MIAMI, FL	4/20	LOUISVILLE, KY
3/9	ST. PETERSBURG, FL	4/22	TOLEDO, OH
3/12	COLUMBIA, SC	4/25	SYRACUSE, NY
3/15	CHARLESTON, SC	4/26	ALBANY, NY
3/16	GREENSBORO, NC	4/27	BUFFALO, NY
3/18	HAMPTON, VA	4/30	PORTLAND, ME
3/19	HERSHEY, PA	5/2	NEW HAVEN, CT
3/22	PITTSBURGH, PA	5/3	WORCESTER, MA
3/23	CHARLESTON, WV	5/4	BALTIMORE, MD

R.I.O.T. Squads needed!

In this manual you have read about how to enlist members in your own R.I.O.T. Squad. We are encouraging you to begin now getting your group together. We want to hear from you as well about what your group is doing and the things that God is accomplishing through your group.

Squad leaders should call 918-496-1891 and update us on your progress. You can also fax your information to 918-496-2553.

If you have:

A)   questions

B)   need materials to help in your R.I.O.T. Squad

C)   want information on taking your squad international with a Teen Mania trip

D)   want to know how to schedule a Pre-Carman crusade rally in association with Teen Mania with your area squads.

It's time to let the Righteous Invasion of Truth begin!

R.I.O.T. Gear

Now you can get yourself equipped with your own personal R.I.O.T. Gear!

Official R.I.O.T. Shirt..$15.00

R.I.O.T. Dog Tag..$5.00

Righteous Invasion of Truth Pin...$5.00

Official R.I.O.T. Cap..$18.00

Call 1-918-250-1529 now and get ready for a Righteous Invasion of Truth!

QTY.	ITEM	SIZE	PRICE	TOTAL

U.S. SHIPPING/HANDLING	**$ 6.00**
OUTSIDE U.S. SHIPPING/HANDLING	**$20.00**
TOTAL AMOUNT DUE	

Name _____

Address _____
CANNOT SHIP TO POST OFFICE BOX

City_____ State____ Zip _____

Phone_____
ALLOW 2-4 WEEKS DELIVERY

Payment Type ☐ Check ☐ Money Order ☐ Visa
☐ MasterCard ☐ Discover ☐ American Express

Credit Card #_____ Exp Date _____

Name on Credit Card_____

Carman Ministries Partner Number: ACI (7/8G)

_ _ _ _ _ _ _ D

ALL OFFERS ARE GOOD WHILE SUPPLIES LAST
PRODUCT DEPARTMENT
C/O CARMAN MINISTRIES
P.O. BOX 701050 • TULSA, OK 74170
(918) 250-1529   FAX (918) 251-4492

EXTREME. MASSIVE. ETERNAL. BLAZING WITH GOD'S POWER.

One word alone can't describe – much less contain – TEEN MANIA. But we do know this . . . The world – maybe even someone you know – is aching . . . yeah, even dying . . . for what TEEN MANIA has to give.

For the past ten years, Ron Luce, the founder of Teen Mania Ministries, and literally thousands of TEEN MANIACS have been blasting hearts loose from their stone-cold foundations and torching them with God's fire. They create a R.I.O.T. wherever they go . . . which is pretty much around the world. **→**

TEEN MANIA

Ministries®

Acquire the Fire regional conventions are held in 25 cities across North America each year. This coming year, more than 100,000 teens are expected to attend them.

Summer missions programs last year took more than 1,800 teens to 15 nations . . . and yet another team took on Acapulco over Christmas break.

And not just for the <u>fun</u> of it – even though a Teen Mania experience just may be the most fun you'll have this decade.

This is for real. We're talking RESULTS. Huge, turn-your-life-around results. Last year, more than 90,000 people accepted Christ as a result of the missions program alone.

Yeah, I guess you could call that a R.I.O.T. Big time.

Tired of mediocrity and the same old ho-hum? Have we got a challenge for you!

Take a look at the countries listed in the box. And then take a look at the application on the next two pages. Pray about the list. Then pick up a pen.

If you want more information about Acquire the Fire youth conventions, or more information about summer missions trips, call **1-800-299-TEEN.**

Ministries®

TAKING THE **R.I.O.T.** INTERNATIONAL

Want to be part of taking your R.I.O.T. into one of these nations? You can be! We're talking serious involvement.

Albania	Ecuador	Morocco
Bolivia	El Salvador	Russia
Botswana	Ghana	Thailand
Cameroon	Hong Kong	Ukraine
China	India	Venezuela

TEEN MANIA "WORLD CHANGER"
APPLICATION

Are you serious about wanting to spread a R.I.O.T. into another nation next summer? Your first step is to fill out the application below and send it in. Be sure to fill out *both* sides!

NAME (AS ON BIRTH CERTIFICATE)
LAST   FIRST   MIDDLE INITIAL

SOCIAL SECURITY NUMBER   ☐ MALE ☐ FEMALE

CITIZEN OF WHAT NATION?   BIRTH DATE   /   /   AGE   HEIGHT   WEIGHT

CURRENT ADDRESS

CITY   STATE   ZIP

HOME PHONE   DAYTIME PHONE
(   )   (

PERMANENT ADDRESS

CITY   STATE   ZIP

HAVE YOU BEEN ON A TEEN MANIA SUMMER MISSIONS TRIP BEFORE? ☐ YES ☐ NO   IF SO, HOW MANY?

NATION   TRIP   YEAR

NATION   TRIP   YEAR

IF YOU ARE IN A DATING RELATIONSHIP WITH SOMEONE, IS THIS PERSON APPLYING TO COME ON A TEEN MANIA MISSIONS TRIP? ☐ YES ☐ NO

IF YES, NAME

COUNTRY

ALL APPLICANTS WILL BE PLACED IN NATIONS BASED ON QUALIFICATIONS, PAST REFERENCES, AVAILABILITY, AND DESIRE. THEREFORE, IT IS POSSIBLE THAT AN APPLICANT MAY NOT BE ACCEPTED TO THE NATION OF CHOICE. PLEASE NOTE THAT ALL TEAM LEADER CANDIDATES ARE PLACED AFTER TEAM LEADER TRAINING CAMP.

CHURCH NAME

PASTOR

CITY

STATE

ZIP

CHURCH PHONE

(   )

HOW LONG HAVE YOU BEEN INVOLVED IN THIS CHURCH?

DATE YOU MADE COMMITMENT TO FOLLOW CHRIST?

/   /

WHICH NATION ARE YOU APPLYING FOR?

FIRST CHOICE:

SECOND CHOICE:

☐ MY APPLICATION FEE OF $39 IS ENCLOSED.

I UNDERSTAND THAT THIS FAST-TRACK APPLICATION WILL BEGIN THE PROCESS BUT THAT THERE WILL BE OTHER INFORMATION I MUST SUPPLY TO TEEN MANIA FOR ACCEPTANCE TO A SUMMER MINISTRY TRIP. I AGREE TO BE BOUND BY ALL THE STANDARD TEEN MANIA SPECIFIC QUALIFICATIONS AS OUTLINED IN THE FINAL APPLICATION PAPERWORK I RECEIVE. I UNDERSTAND THAT MY $39 APPLICATION FEE IS NONREFUNDABLE.

SIGNATURE

SEND THIS FAST-TRACK APPLICATION WITH YOUR APPLICATION FEE TO:

TEEN MANIA MINISTRIES
P.O. BOX 700721
TULSA, OK 74170-0721